Take Back Your Time: 101 Simple Tips To Shrink Your Work-Week and Conquer the Chaos in Your Life

SHARI MCGUIRE

Roy -
To taking back
your time.
Shari McGuire

ISBN: 978-0-9849712-0-6

DEDICATION

This book is dedicated to my incredible husband and best friend Jim.

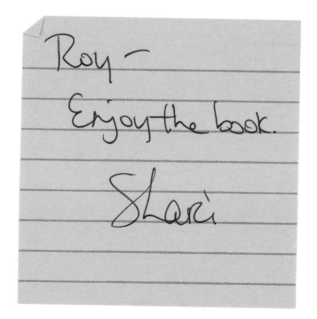

CONTENTS

ACKNOWLEDGMENTS

I wish to say a very special, "I couldn't have done it without you" thank you to my coach Kathy Eppley.

I also wish to personally thank Steven Bolster and Kari Beth Krieger for respectively lending their professional journalism skills and editing skills to this book.

1 INTRODUCTION

Time management isn't about managing time, it's about modifying your behavior to make the most of the 24 hours a day each of us is given. That's 168 hours per week and 8760 hours in a year.

Ever wonder how some people seem to pull off an amazing amount of accomplishments in a year while others barely have anything to show for their time on this planet?

If you sat down at the end of the year to write a year in review letter, would it be jam-packed with things you set as goals that you've accomplished or would all of your accomplishments still be on your wish list?

If your tendency is more toward a wish list of unaccomplished goals, this book is a great tool to get you started moving in the right direction and I'm excited about the journey you are about to embark on.

Enjoy this book as much as I enjoyed writing it for you. I hope you'll find, as I have, that time management can be fun and easy if you break it down into 101 pieces.

2 HOW TO USE THIS BOOK

Though I would prefer to see you read every page of this book, you will most likely just flip through it to find tips that strike you. And that's OK. Keep the book with you for a while and see how the tips in this book help you to take back your time and enjoy more free time than you thought possible.

As you read, you might think of things you would have included in this book. Email your ideas to 101Tips@ShrinkYourWorkWeek.com and I might include them with your name in the next edition of this book.

All The Best,

Shari McGuire

3 PRIORITIZE

"If you want to make good use of your time, you've got to know what's most important and then give it all you've got."

-- Lee Iacocca

Tip 1.

For two days or a week, whichever you prefer, log exactly how you're spending your time in your current routine for all waking hours. All waking hours is important if you are someone who brings work out at night or if you want to improve your time management at home in addition to work. At the end of your logging period you will have a very clear understanding of how you typically spend your time and will begin to understand where adjustments can be made for better productivity and work life balance.

Tip 2.

Keep track of the time it takes for you to do each of your tasks. Use that information to schedule an appropriate block of time to complete the task in the future.

Tip 3.

The Pareto Principle reminds us to identify the 20 percent of our activities that produce 80 percent of our results and concentrate on that 20 percent first. To accomplish this, at the start of your day, ask yourself, "What are the three things I must get done today that fall in my 20 percent?" Then block time on your calendar to accomplish each of those things today.

Tip 4.

When the fire drills of the day begin to consume your time, remind yourself of the 20 percent you need to focus on. If something in the schedule has to slip, if something isn't going to get done, make sure it's not part of that 20 percent.

Tip 5.

Categorize each task in your task list so you can easily group like items together. For example, I start tasks that are phone calls with the word "Call," offline tasks I need to complete start with "Desk" and Internet research tasks I need to do start with "Online."

Tip 6.

Further prioritize your tasks into one of these four categories in this order of importance:

1. urgent and important,
2. not urgent but important,
3. urgent but not important, and
4. not urgent and not important.

Tip 7.

Do like tasks together. For example, make all of your phone calls together, run all of your errands together, or write thank you cards to customers together. Combine this tip with Tip 5 for even more power and time management efficiency.

4 MANAGE YOUR SCHEDULE

"Don't be fooled by the calendar. There are only as many days in the year as you make use of. One man gets only a week's value out of a year while another man gets a full year's value out of a week."

-- Charles Richards

Tip 8.

Include your personal office hours in your email signature and adhere to them – meaning if you say you're done at 4:30, leave the office at 4:30. Treat your ending time with the same respect and courtesy you would extend if there were another person waiting for you to leave.

Tip 9.

Create appointments with yourself -- set aside blocks of time to achieve specific tasks. I like to call this creating a standardized schedule. For example, if you always need to deliver a status report on Wednesday morning, block out time on your calendar every Tuesday to write your status report and you'll always have time set aside to achieve that task during your work day.

Tip 10.

Over time, cut five to ten minutes off every block of time scheduled for tasks.   Albert Einstein said, "Time is only an illusion." What he meant is that we expand or contract our work to fill the time available. By allowing a little less time, tasks still get accomplished, and you'll have "free" time at the end of the day to get a head start on tomorrow's schedule, spend more time with your family or friends, or just take a breath!

Tip 11.

Treat the appointments you've created with yourself to get things done with the same respect and courtesy you would extend if there were another person present. Don't get distracted by "shiny objects" such as new email arriving, the telephone ringing or a co-worker stopping by.

Tip 12.

Schedule and eat your live frog first. Mark Twain said, "Eat a live frog first thing in the morning and nothing worse will happen to you the rest of the day." The live frog task is the task you're most likely to procrastinate and it may even have the most positive impact on your life or provide the biggest results in your business. By scheduling your "live frog" task first in your day then you'll be done with it and can move on to other tasks.

Tip 13.

Focus on one task at a time. Multitasking kills your productivity as it can take 20-40 percent more time to finish a list of tasks when you multitask, compared with completing the same list of tasks in sequence.

Tip 14.

Break large, time-consuming tasks into smaller tasks. This serves several purposes. First, it enables you to break the task down into accomplishable steps and increases your likelihood of completing the overall task. This is like the metaphor of how do you eat an elephant - one bite at a time. Second, you can see the steps that are achievable now and schedule in the future the subsequent steps.

For example, let's say you need to replace the glass in your china hutch. First, you need to measure for the size of glass you need; Second, you need to research where to purchase the glass; Third, you need to purchase the glass; and Fourth, you need to install the glass. From there you can see that today you can do steps one and two, tomorrow when you run errands you can do step three and this weekend you can do step four.

Tip 15.

Before you set up a new meeting, ask yourself if you can accomplish your agenda without a meeting or in an already scheduled meeting.

Tip 16.

Include an agenda in your meeting request. Then you and the attendees know what you want to accomplish and attendees will have enough information to come prepared to your meeting or self-select out if it doesn't apply to them.

Tip 17.

Know when you are most productive and schedule time to work on your most difficult tasks then.

Tip 18.

To see if you really need a meeting, cancel it. See if you can find a more effective way to accomplish the agenda you had planned for the meeting.

5 CALL IN REINFORCEMENTS

"One always has time enough, if one will apply it well."

-- Johann Wolfgang von Goethe

Tip 19.

What work are you doing in your business or job that can be more productively outsourced or delegated? Do you enjoy those tasks and are you good at them? Do they fit in your 20 percent parameter (see Pareto Principle in Tip 3)? How much time does it take you to complete them? Are there other activities that would be a better use of your time? If so, hire someone to do the work for you (e.g., a bookkeeper or virtual assistant) or delegate to someone on your staff. Even if you don't own your own business or have staff, you can still find creative ways to delegate.

For example, in my corporate job, there are key players who write documents for projects I lead. When those documents were ready for sign-off by the larger project team, I used to manage the collection of signatures on the documents on behalf of those key players. I have since trained those key players how to obtain the signatures themselves, which took a huge weight off my to do list to have more time to focus on higher value tasks.

Tip 20.

Train your employees adequately. A big time drain for business owners is an employee who constantly asks questions, interrupting their day. If this is happening to you, the problem may be that the employee is not adequately trained to do their job.

Tip 21.

Create a "Frequently Asked Questions" section and display it prominently on your website to help your customers answer their own questions and reduce the number of calls to you or your staff.

Tip 22.

Hang back and resist the impulse to jump in every time an employee encounters difficulty. Making mistakes is a great teacher and saves you time when you're not rescuing your staff as they will more quickly become independent.

6 COMMAND RESPECT FOR YOUR SCHEDULE

"Until you value yourself, you will not value your time. Until you value your time, you will not do anything with it."

-- M. Scott Peck

Tip 23.

Let's say you leave the office at 5 p.m. Your boss has scheduled a meeting to last until 5 p.m. and he is notorious for exceeding the allotted time. Before the meeting starts, let your boss know that you have a prior commitment (even if you don't have an appointment – your commitment is to yourself that you leave at 5 p.m.) and need to leave promptly at 5 p.m. Then walk out of the meeting guilt free at 5 p.m. if he goes over. Your boss will respect you for it and your colleagues will be green with envy wishing they had done the same.

Tip 24.

Ten minutes before a meeting is scheduled to end, evaluate what's left on your agenda with the people in the meeting. Decide with the people are meeting with if you can finish the conversation now or if a follow up meeting is necessary. If a follow-up is necessary, schedule it before time runs out.

Tip 25.

Let's say your work hours are 8:00 a.m. - 4:30 p.m. Block your calendar as busy from 4:30 p.m. – 8:00 a.m. every day so people won't expect you to attend a meeting during that time.

Tip 26.

If someone does schedule a meeting during your non-work hours, respond with a "sorry, my office hours are 8:00 a.m. - 4:30 p.m., if you need me to participate in the meeting, please reschedule for a time during my working hours, otherwise I will review the meeting minutes when distributed."

Tip 27.

Similarly, let's say you've blocked your calendar to leave early today to go to a doctor appointment or watch your child's basketball game and someone schedules a meeting during that time. Simply decline the meeting, indicating you have a prior commitment for that time slot. Ask them to reschedule for a time you are free or to proceed without you and you will read the meeting minutes. Don't explain why you need to leave because that opens the door for others to pass judgment on your decision to leave.

Tip 28.

Confirm your priorities with your boss. Make sure what you're working on is of the highest priority to your boss and pace yourself to complete the project or task during your normal business hours. There's nothing worse than pulling an all-nighter for a project your boss didn't need for another week.

Tip 29.

Train your colleagues to answer their own questions whenever possible and to come to you only when your help is truly needed. Let's say you receive a request for a copy of a document that will be reviewed in a meeting tomorrow. You've already shared a copy of the document with the requestor and they've chosen the easy way out to ask you for a copy again. Resist the urge to waste your time in locating the document and re-sending it to them. Instead, politely say, "I attached a copy of it in the meeting notice for tomorrow. Please let me know if you don't see it."

Tip 30.

Train your subordinates and colleagues to propose solutions when they raise an issue to you. If you always ask, "What do you think our options are and our best solution is?" it won't take long for them to realize they need to bring options and a proposed solution if they raise an issue to you.

Tip 31.

The next time you have a short agenda for your meeting and you want to keep it that way, move the chairs to the side and ask people to stand. Your request signals to the group that this is going to be a quick and focused meeting.

Tip 32.

Stand up the next time you're talking on the telephone. Not only will it improve blood flow to your brain and thus improve your thinking, you'll find the conversation will be shorter.

7 RESPECT YOUR SCHEDULE

"It's how we spend our time here and now, that really matters. If you are fed up with the way you have come to interact with time, change it."

-- Marcia Wieder

Tip 33.

Create a reading file of letters, memos, reports, clipped newspaper articles or clipped magazine articles. When you are stuck in traffic, early to a meeting or sitting in a doctor's office, pull out your file and read something meaningful to pass the time.

Tip 34.

Plan ahead for those times when you'll have a few extra minutes. Such as arriving at a meeting early or

Tip 35.

Maintain control of your free time. Do not scan email during the evenings or weekend. You have earned the time away from work and you may see an email that you can't resolve until the next workday anyway and you may find yourself dwelling on the issue.

Tip 36.

Sometimes people will ask you to complete a task that just isn't a good use of your time and yet our tendency is to oblige. Instead, say, "I can help you by finding out who really should be doing this," or, "How about if I show you how to do that and then you'll be all set to go."

Tip 37.

You can't always say no, but you can you can take control by establishing your terms. For example you can say, "OK, I think I can squeeze that in. I expect I'll be able to get it to you by three o'clock today. Does that work?" When you set the schedule rather than letting someone set it for you, you maintain control and can better manage your time.

Tip 38.

Consider putting a tough condition on your agreement. "If it would only take an hour, I'd be able to help, but I can't give you more than that." When in doubt, it's easier to say no now, and then change your mind to a yes later, rather than the other way around. People will respect you more for having the courage to say no or set a limit than when you say yes and fail to follow thr

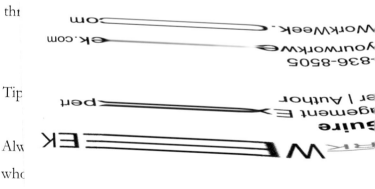

Tip

Alw

who those who are late by waiting for them. Do something, however minor, but get started.

Tip 40.

Schedule your meetings to start five minutes after the hour to give people a chance to finish their prior meeting, take a break and get to your meeting on time. This works amazingly well. Also always end your meetings on time. You'll save significant amounts of time! And people will appreciate you for it.

Tip 41.

If you really want to live a more balanced life, start by looking at the choices you are making. Resolve today to stop blaming others or circumstances for a lack of balance and instead, look within yourself first and decide what it is you really want out of life.

Tip 42.

Commit to do just one thing this week or weekend to begin to put balance back in your life. Call a friend, go to a movie with your family, buy a book, sign up for that course you've been putting off, schedule a golf game or spend the day working on your favorite craft. Do this every week for a year and you'll be amazed at all the life you've put back in your days.

Tip 43.

Follow the old saying; "Any job worth doing, is worth doing well." Doing work right the first time may take more time initially and yet it results in less time spent making corrections on the back end, which saves you more time overall.

Tip 44.

If you're fairly certain a meeting will just take 15 minutes, schedule it only for 15 minutes. Because calendaring programs default to 30-minute meetings, the tendency is to unnecessarily book the full 30-minutes. I have news for you. Time expands and contracts to fit the time we have allotted to a task. When we allot 30 minutes to a 15-minute task, we will find a way to use all 30 minutes and now you've lost 15 minutes in your day, which adds up fast. When you save yourself 15 minutes every business day in a year, assuming you work 48 weeks after vacation and holidays that's 60 hours you've just put back in your life!

8 STREAMLINE TO GAIN EFFICIENCY

"Time = Life; therefore, waste your time and waste your life, or master your time and master your life."

-- Alan Lakein

Tip 45.

Create logical folders on your computer to keep your files organized and easy to find in the future. The best time to file a document is the first time you save it. You might group files based on a project, client name or place all performance reviews in a Performance Review folder with each year as a subfolder.

Tip 46.

If you own a business, get a separate bank account for your business and use is. A business bank account will save you time as you won't need to sort through transactions in your personal account to find business expenses.

Tip 47.

Streamline tasks and activities that you do over and over again. Whether it be creating a status report or mailing a client thank you letter. Detail out the steps you follow to complete the tasks and ask yourself, "How can I be more efficient in completing these tasks?"

Tip 48.

Also cut out frivolous tasks and activities that don't add value and only take up more time. Periodically ask yourself, "What is the value this activity adds? Does it help me meet my goals and objectives?" Just because you've been generating a report every week for the last five years doesn't mean that it's an effective use of time. If the activity is frivolous, stop doing it and see if anyone misses it. I've found more often than not that no one even notices.

Tip 49.

Five minutes before every telephone call, whether it be one on one or a conference call with a lot of people, pause and ask yourself what result you want to attain from the call and gather the information you need for your meeting. This will help you know what success for that telephone call looks like before you start. Then, after each telephone call, assess whether your desired result was achieved. If not, what happened? What do you still need? How can you efficiently get that information? What can you do different next time to achieve your desired result?

Tip 50.

Stop automatically attending all the meetings you're invited to. When you receive a meeting invitation ask yourself, "What is the agenda for this meeting? Do any of the agenda items pertain to me? Can I get what I need out of the meeting if I just read the meeting minutes? Can I send someone in my place?" If you can just read the minutes, let the organizer know you will not attend and look forward to reviewing the minutes. If you can send someone in your place, forward the invitation to him or her and ask that they report back to you with information you need to know after the meeting.

Tip 51.

Create and use templates for documents and presentations you regularly generate such as new business pitches, meeting agendas or monthly financial reports.

Tip 52.

Remove items on your task list that consistently remain at the bottom and will realistically never get done. These tasks weigh you down mentally because you are reminded again and again that those tasks never seem to get completed and you will feel discouraged.

9 MANAGE YOUR EMAIL, DON'T LET IT MANAGE YOU

"Time is what we want most, but what we use worst."

-- William Penn

Tip 53.

Create an email subject line code and include the definition in your email so people know how best to respond to your email. For example, I use "RR" for response requested, "RO" for read only, "AR" to indicate I need you to take an action before responding and "FYI" as informational only. Include those definitions in a key within your email signature.

Tip 54.

Schedule a block or two of time during the day to review and answer email, your volume of email will dictate frequency and how long to read email. I schedule a 45-minute session to review email in the morning and an hour session mid-day. Communicate that to your audience in your email signature to set expectations with them. Here is the exact verbiage from my email signature: "I set aside 7:15 a.m. - 8:00 a.m. CT and 12:00 p.m. - 1:00 p.m. CT every day to read and respond to emails. As time permits I also glance through my emails throughout the day. If you require urgent assistance (please ensure it is urgent) that cannot wait until 7:15 a.m. CT or 12 p.m. CT, please contact me via phone at xxx-xxx-xxxx. Thank you for understanding this move to more efficiency and effectiveness. It helps me accomplish more to serve you better. "

Tip 55.

You may also want to create an auto-responder as new email comes in to thank the sender for their email and alert them to your email review process (see Tip 54). People will respect you for it and know when to expect a reply from you.

Tip 56.

Set email you send to deliver in the future when others aren't answering to prevent email chat back and forth.

Tip 57.

Use consistent subject lines in your emails so people know what you are writing about. For example, if your email is about a particular project, put the name of the project in the email in addition to a description specific to your email topic.

Tip 58.

Write meaningful subject lines (for example, don't reply to a random email with a completely unrelated topic) and change the subject line if the email has become a chain of emails and the topic has now shifted.

Tip 59.

When replying "thank you" or writing a very brief email (one sentence), put the thank you or brief sentence in the subject with EOM (End Of Message) at the end. People will know that is the end of the message and there is no need to open your email. I would suggest adding EOM to your key in your email signature (see Tip 53 for more on creating a key).

Tip 60.

When you receive junk email, don't even open them. Delete them immediately. They are well designed marketing ploys that will suck you in and waste your time! The emails could also contain a virus that could infect your computer, wasting even more time.

Tip 61.

If you trust the sender of a junk email, an option is to open it and scroll to the bottom of the email – don't waste your time reading any of the email – and click on unsubscribe so you don't receive emails from that sender any more.

Tip 62.

If you're like me, you love to get sales and other announcements from businesses that can quickly clutter your Inbox (if you work for a corporation, I recommend receiving these emails in your personal Inbox). For those emails, create a folder called "retailers" (or whatever makes sense to you). Then, for all of the senders of this category of emails, create a rule to place emails from the sender in your retailers folder. When you're ready to shop at a particular retailer, check the retailers folder to see if they have a current sale promotion.

Tip 63.

Every two weeks, delete emails in your "retailers" folder that are 14 days old or older (see Tip 62). Those emails will contain expired offers and quickly become clutter if not purged.

Tip 64.

Turn off new email notifications so you're not distracted by the visual cue or sound that new mail has arrived.

Tip 65.

Think of key people whose emails you would like to have stand out from the crowd in your Inbox. Create rules to color code emails that come in from those individuals. For example, blue from your boss and green from key customers. Then you can quickly scan through your emails to find those that are most critical to respond to quickly.

Tip 66.

If you are having difficultly composing an email, it usually suggests that a higher order of communication such as a telephone call or face-to-face meeting is necessary. Abandon your email and either call the recipient or set up a meeting with him.

Tip 67.

Pick up the phone to save time over sending an email or instant message. Communication is clearer and crisper over the phone and it's faster to "get on the same" page in a live conversation than it is via email or an instant message.

Tip 68.

If you need someone to answer a question right away, don't send an email hoping she'll see it instantly and promptly respond to you. Just call her.

Tip 69.

Move emails directly from your Inbox to your calendar and schedule a block of time to complete the request in the email. This saves you time as you won't need to add it to a task list and you'll remember at an appropriate time in the future to complete the request.

Tip 70.

Close your email when concentrating on a project so you're not tempted to peek and see if new emails have arrived. Distractions cost you 20 minutes of lost productivity per interruption.

BONUS

Get my **6 Secret Steps To An Empty Inbox** when you go to www.shrinkyourworkweek.com/inbox.

---

10 CREATE REALISTIC DEADLINES AND EXTINGUISH FIRE DRILLS

"It's not enough to be busy, so are the ants. The question is, what are we busy about?"

-- Henry David Thoreau

Tip 71.

When someone requests your assistance on a task, ask for a deadline. Chances are you may assume they need it right away and in reality they may not need it for another week, or at least a couple of days. Without asking for a deadline, you may drop everything to unnecessarily get it done today.

Tip 72.

When someone asks you to complete a task in an unrealistic timeframe, counter with a deadline in which you can realistically accomplish the full task. If the task can be split, offer completion of the most critical piece of the task by the originally requested deadline. Often the task is suddenly less urgent when you respectfully counter with a realistic deadline.

Tip 73.

Here's another option when a superior asks you to do something and they're relentless on it needing to be completed immediately. Reply with "I'm happy to get as much of the task completed for you today before I leave for a prior commitment at 4 p.m. Doing so will cause me to set aside Project ABC which I had planned to work on today. Will that be agreeable to you?" With this response you've stood your ground to leave on time (regardless of what your plans are after work) and given the requestor the choice of which task takes precedence.

Tip 74.

Give people an arbitrary deadline to set yourself up for success – if you need something first thing on a Wednesday, ask for it by Noon on Tuesday and set a reminder for yourself to ask for it again if Tuesday at Noon comes and goes and you haven't received the information you requested.

Tip 75.

Better yet, assign a deadline to the email you send requesting the information so the person you're requesting the information from gets a pop up message on their computer reminding them to complete the assignment.

11 REMOVE DISTRACTIONS

"One worthwhile task carried to a successful conclusion is worth half-a-hundred half-finished tasks."

-- Malcolm S. Forbes

Tip 76.

Turn off or put instant messaging software on "do not disturb." Did you know that you lose 20 minutes of productivity for every interruption in your day? Getting "pinged" just three times a day causes you to lose an hour of productivity. Take those three hours times five days in a week, times 48 work weeks in a year, that's 720 hours of lost productivity annually. What could you accomplish with 720 hours a year?

Tip 77.

When the telephone rings and you are deep in thought on a project or activity, don't answer it. Remember the 20 minutes of lost productivity I mentioned? This applies here as well. To prevent the distraction of the phone ringing, you could unplug it or have it roll directly to voicemail.

Consider setting a reminder on your calendar to turn your phone back on upon completion of your project or activity.

Tip 78.

Change your voicemail to set expectations with people who call so they know when you are free to call them back. For example, "Hi, this is Sara Stewart. Today is Monday the fifth and I will be in meetings from 8:00 a.m. to 10:00 a.m. and from 1:00 p.m. to 3:00 p.m. I will be returning calls between 11:00 a.m. and 12:00 p.m. and again between 4:00 p.m. and 5:00 p.m. Please leave your name and a number where you can be reached during those hours. I look forward to speaking with you." People who leave messages will appreciate knowing when they can expect a call back from you.

Tip 79.

Stay organized. I know that can be a tall order. Many studies have proven that disorganization in an office leads to a great deal of wasted time. Time is wasted when you constantly have to dig through piles of paper on your desk to find the right document, search your hard drive for that report you wrote or wonder where you put the stamps. Keeping your desktop, supplies and computer files organized will allow you more time to focus only upon the task at hand. Each time you find yourself distracted by disorganization, file as many papers as you can in the next two minutes. Eventually, the disorganization will disappear.

Tip 80.

Clean your desk at the end of each day and create tasks or calendar items of what needs to be accomplished the next day. That will cut down on wasted time each morning sorting through what needs to be accomplished.

Tip 81.

If you struggle with cleaning your desk every day, set aside one to two hours every Friday to participate in Scoop Your Desk Fridays. I used to get to the end of a week and have piles of papers and post it notes everywhere. So, I invented Scoop Your Desk Fridays where I literally scooped everything into a pile and went through the papers one by one throwing away what was no longer needed, filing what could be filed and writing tasks on my calendar or to do list for tasks that had been assigned to me. Over time, my time management skills have improved greatly so I no longer need to do this. Stick with it and you will experience the same result.

Tip 82.

When you need to uninterrupted time to work on a project or task, establish a visual cue to communicate to people that you can't be disturbed. Several ideas are to close your office door or to put up a "please do not disturb" sign. You can either make your own sign or purchase a retractable message banner on the Internet.

12 MORE FREE TIME AT HOME

"The key is in not spending time, but in investing it."

-- Stephen R. Covey

Tip 83.

Create bins in your closet to presort laundry. I have a bin for each of the following categories: cold/white, cold/color, warm/white and warm/color. Then, as clothes get soiled, in the correct bin they go. This makes it super fast and easy to create a load of laundry, especially when you've got to get your favorite blouse washed for an important meeting tomorrow.

Tip 84.

With caller ID today, we know who is calling before we answer the phone so don't answer the sales call that comes in the middle of your dinner or any call that comes at any time that would be disruptive to what you have occurring in your home.

Setting a different ring tones for important callers can also help you quickly determine whether or not to answer the phone.

Tip 85.

Or, if your phone rings and you know it's a sales call and it won't disrupt your day too much to pick up the phone, kindly cut into the sales-pitch and state, "please put me on your do not call list."

Tip 86.

Do one better, get rid of your landline phone and go with just your cell phone and you won't be on any calling lists unless you give out your phone number. Have a big house? No problem, buy a cordless phone system that is compatible with Bluetooth®-enabled cell phones and your cell phone will ring throughout your home.

Tip 87.

As your mail comes in your home each day, set it in a designated spot. Then, once a week go through the whole stack at once. This allows you to "get in a groove" and quickly sort through your mail.

Tip 88.

Put your bills on auto pay or set them up in your online banking program to be paid through your banks website automatically every month. We get to pay our bills anyway each month; just let your creditors come in and collect what's owed them with no extra effort on your part. Why waste your time with something as mundane and boring as paying bills? Not to mention the fees and damage to your credit report that go along with missing a payment.

Tip 89.

Set personal goals. Personal goal setting is essential to managing your time well because goals give you a destination and vision to work toward. Do you know what you want your life to look like in six months?

One year? Three years? Ten years? If you don't, how will you get there? Goals help you decide what's worth spending your time on vs. what are distractions that prevent you from living the life you dream of.

Tip 90.

Cut out two things in your life that aren't fulfilling to you. Ask yourself, on a scale of 1 to 10 with 10 being the highest and best, how excited and motivated am I to do this activity? If you don't rank it at least an 8, stop doing it. This frees up time in your day to focus on activities that you are most passionate about.

Tip 91.

A lot of time is wasted searching through stacks of papers, overflowing cupboards and other chaos in our homes. Spend some time clearing the clutter in your life and you'll free up lots of time in your schedule because you'll know where to go the next time you need something and you won't have to sort through junk you don't use. When I clear clutter, I like to sort it into three piles: keep, donate and trash. After an initial sort, go through the keep pile again to sort things further to particular rooms in your home they belong in and then you can easily carry each pile to the room where it belongs – and put them away immediately. If you've got enough space and baskets or containers, consider sorting the keep pile by room the first pass through to save additional time.

Tip 92.

Turn off the television. I'm serious. How much TV do you watch in a week? Are you living the life you dream of or are you complaining that there aren't enough hours in the day? What if you didn't watch TV, how many more hours would you have in a week or year to accomplish your goals? What if you just gained 3 hours each week – that's 156 hours in a year! If you must watch TV, pre-record your favorite shows so you can fast forward over the commercials and reduce the amount of time it takes to watch your shows. Watching shows on Hulu and network websites are also good options time saving options.

Tip 93.

Save up your errands and then create a plan to accomplish them in the shortest time possible. To do that, make a list of all the errands you need to run, writing the store names as headers. Then, sort the stores by geographical location (meaning find the store closest to your home) and write a number '1' by it. Then find the next closest store and write a number '2' by it and so on. Then attend to your errands in the order you just created and you'll get your errands done in no time.

If your errand list is too long for the block of time you have available, follow your list through as many stops as you can make and then pick up where you left off the next time.

Tip 94.

Designate a place you always put key objects that tend to get lost – for example:

- I have mini-hooks on the inside of our mudroom door where I hang my car keys as I walk in the door.
- I set my purse in the same spot every day when I get home, immediately plug in my cell phone and set my phone on top of my purse so I remember my phone the next time I leave the house.

13 TIME MANAGEMENT FOR PARENTS AND THEIR CHILDREN

"You will never find time for anything. If you want time, you must make it."

-- Charles Bruxton

Tip 95.

Set a schedule with your children's input and hold everyone accountable to keeping it. For example, if you collectively decide that breakfast is served from 6:30 – 6:45 a.m., anyone showing up for breakfast and consuming it during that time gets to eat breakfast. If a family member is late for breakfast (Mom and Dad too!), he or she doesn't get to eat breakfast and time marches on to the next thing on your schedule. This may sound harsh, it gets you out the door on time though and I bet they'll only miss breakfast once.

Tip 96.

Stop nagging. When you train your children to know that it takes three reminders from you before they really need to complete a task, they will wait for the third reminder. Set the expectation up front (you've got 10 minutes to get dressed) and allow them to succeed or fail and own their results. Even small children can learn to manage their time by setting a timer.

Tip 97.

Incorporate preparing for the next morning into everyone's bedtime routine (Mom and Dad too!). Make everyone's lunches, pack backpacks and briefcases so they're ready to go, sign paperwork for field trips, etc. In addition, set everything in a consistent spot in your home so it's easy to remember on the way out the door.

Also consider setting aside healthy grab and go breakfasts.

Tip 98.

Organize hand-me-downs by keeping them sorted in bins by size and season so you can easily pull out only the clothes that will fit next. For example, let's say your child is now in a size 6 and it's winter. Pull out the bin of size 6 clothes for winter and you have an instant wardrobe. You won't need to waste your time looking through too big clothes and, if your child skips a size, just set that bin aside for donation or a garage sale.

Tip 99.

When you have a big job to do around the house, hire a babysitter to watch your children (preferably out of the house) so you can get the job done faster. For example, when my husband I and cleaned out our basement to prepare for finishing it we took our then 2 ½ year old son to an hourly day care. He had a blast at day care and we breezed through the cleaning effort without his "help."

Or, if you have relatives handy set up your child for a play date at their home.

Tip 100.

Spend time teaching your children how to do tasks around the home. It can often seem easier to do things yourself, but in the long run this is not going to give you any more time. By spending time teaching children to do simple tasks for themselves, not only will you increase their self-confidence as you build their independence, it will also eventually free up some time for yourself, as you will not have to do this task for them. Start with small things like tying their own shoelaces, making their bed and making a sandwich.

Tip 101.

Keep a stash of non-perishable healthy snacks in your car so if you're running errands or to and from an activity when it's snack time you won't need to make a stop somewhere for food. This also works well when it's mealtime. The snacks in your car will tide your kids over until you can get home and prepare a meal.

ABOUT THE AUTHOR

Shari McGuire is founder of ShrinkYourWorkWeek.com and is a Time Management, Productivity and Profitability expert.

She has more than 20 years experience guiding large corporations and individuals in strategies and techniques to more efficiently manage their time, which improves profitability and provides balance in their lives.

Shari has been a blogger in <u>Identity Magazine</u> and on <u>Yahoo</u> and is quoted in <u>Redbook, Phoenix Focus, The Grindstone</u> and the book <u>Ignited: Managers! Light Up Your Company and Career for More Power, More Purpose and More Success</u> by Vince Thompson.

She lives in Maple Grove, Minnesota with her husband Jim, son Trevor and dog Bailey.

THANK YOU FOR CHOOSING TO TAKE BACK YOUR TIME.

Here's A Gift For You.

Instant access to a free seminar where you can learn how you too can find 1200 hours in your year and have more time in your day than you imagined. Find 1200 hours in your year and have more time in your day than you imagined.

Feel free to share this gift with friends and family.

www.shrinkyourworkweek.com/gift